Alina: The White Lady of Oystermouth

Ann Marie Thomas

Alina Publishing
Swansea

Published by Alina Publishing
45 Rhondda Street, Mount Pleasant,
Swansea SA1 6ER

ISBN: 978-0-9571988-0-7

Printed by
Brynymor Digital Press

Illustrations by Carrie Francis

Contents

Connect with the author online:

Alina blog: https://alinathewhitelady.wordpress.com/ - for the process of writing this book and news of publicity and future work on this topic.
Personal blog: https://annmariethinkingoutloud.wordpress.com/ - thinking about a lot of things, but especially my faith and my writing - mostly poetry and science fiction.
Twitter: @AnnMThomas80 - on writing
Facebook: https://www.facebook.com/pages/Alina-The-White-Lady-of-Oystermouth/160902344026965
Email: mailto:amt.tetelestai@gmail.com

The book is also available as an ebook, with more chapters of background information but no endnotes, which don't work in ebook format. Buy the book in multiple formats on Smashwords: http://www.smashwords.com/profile/view/alinadebreos, and from Amazon for Kindle.

Introduction

In Swansea town centre you will find Castle Square, a large open space used for events like concerts and markets. On the eastern side of the square stand the ruins of Swansea Castle, but what remains marks the site of what, in 1300, was called the New Castle. The New Castle was created from the south eastern corner of the original castle.

The original stone castle enclosed a large part of what is now the town centre, with many plots of land rented to burgesses and other tenants inside the walls.[1] It was one of the largest castles in South Wales.[2] Castle Square was then the open area inside the castle, called the bailey, where a regular market was held.[3]

Swansea today is the second city of Wales, after Cardiff, but at that time it was the capital of the Lordship of Gower. The Lordship of Gower covered far more than the peninsular of Gower today. The land above the peninsular was also included, all the way from Loughor in the west to the River Tawe in the east, and north to the River Amman. This was not a very important lordship, and Swansea's main significance was as a shipping centre and the main crossing point for the River Tawe. But you may be surprised to learn that the heir to Swansea Castle in 1320 was pivotal in the rebellion which overthrew the king of England.

The heir to Swansea Castle at that time was Alina de Breos and her husband John de Mowbray, and their problems were caused by Alina's father, William de Breos. I am using the life of Alina de Breos to tell this story, as it is through Alina that we can examine the actions of both her father and her husband.

At the time Alina was born, the 'New Castle' had not yet been built, and the Old Castle, with its battle damage from attacks by the Welsh, was probably not very good to live in. Once the 'New Castle' was built we do have evidence that the castle was used in the early 14th century, as there are documents issued to William de Breos there.[4] But for most of the time the family preferred to live at Oystermouth Castle, six miles away in Mumbles.

After her many trials and tribulations described in this book, Alina regained Oystermouth Castle and spent the last years of her life there. Tradition has it that she built the chapel block, three storeys high, which can still be seen today. The first floor was residential, with the chapel above. It has carved pieces brought from Neath Abbey and lavish tracery windows rimmed with Sutton stone dressings.[5] People claim to have seen her ghost there, and call her the White Lady of Oystermouth.

Chapter 1 - Beginning

Alina de Breos - referred to in *The Complete Peerage* as Aline de Breuse[6] - was born in 1291, the youngest of three children. Her father was William de Breos, Lord of Gower in South Wales and Bramber[7] in West Sussex, and her mother was Agnes, of whom nothing is known. Alina was named after her father's mother, Alina, the daughter of Thomas de Multon, Lord of Gilsland.[8]

This was obviously an aristocratic family, however, although William was Lord of Gower, the family were not Welsh. Gower was part of the March of Wales and for a long time the March was part of England. The March of Wales referred to the south and east of Wales, which were ruled by the Norman lords, still in charge over two hundred years after William the Conqueror.[9] The Norman conquest of the whole of Wales took over two hundred years, owing to the difficulties of the terrain and the stubbornness of the Welsh resistance.[10]

William inherited the estates from his father, another William (1220-1291)[11], in the same year that Alina was born, but he had been running the estates for some years as his father's health deteriorated.[12] Yet, less than 80 years earlier, the de Breoses had held many more estates, especially in Wales. In the early years of the reign of King John, a previous William de Breos (d.1211) was one of the king's intimate circle, and his holdings included Gower, Kington, Glamorgan, Monmouth, Limerick in Ireland, and estates in England and Normandy. He became one of the richest and most influential men at court. But in the intervening period the estates had all been lost, except Gower and Bramber.[13]

When Alina was born, the family were in difficult financial circumstances, due to mismanagement, scheming and the cost of providing men for the king's wars. Yet Gower was one of the richest of the Marcher lordships. In 1316 it was recorded as being worth £300 (£100,000 today) a year.[14] Unfortunately William inherited not only his father's estates but also his lawsuits and apparent inability to handle money.[15] The lawsuits and debts from William's father were added to by William himself. As early as 1292, the king warned William that if he did not pay his debts, the king's agents would enter Gower and take away his goods.[16]

William sold off many of his possessions to raise money, year after year. It is estimated that William sold off four times as many possessions as his father had done. Most of these sales were made without the king's permission, which should have been sought first. When his wife Agnes died, he married an heiress, Elizabeth de Sully, in 1317, but it does not appear to have resolved his financial problems.

In addition, William had to bear the cost of fighting for the king in Wales, Scotland and Flanders. He was rewarded for service in Flanders by being allowed to purchase the wardship of John de Mowbray, 2nd Baron de Mowbray, who was under age when his father died in 1297.[17] Alina was immediately betrothed to him and they were married in Swansea Castle in 1298,[18] when she was seven and John was twelve.

This was quite unusual, as girls could be betrothed at a young age but were not normally married before the age of twelve, and the betrothal was a big ceremony in itself, intended to stand for several years before the marriage. In fact, a marriage could be annulled if the bride was under twelve or the groom under fourteen.[19] Her father would probably have required special permission for the marriage, but no record has been found. Her father never did pay the five hundred mark fee for their marriage.[20]

It is unlikely that they set up their own household at such a young age, but it is not known when they would have been considered old enough. Certainly the marriage would not have been consummated for some years. John would have come of age when he was twenty one, although he was serving the king long before that.

Alina's family would want to keep up appearances but life would be difficult with the lack of money and I'm sure Alina's mother feared that William would go too far, as had more than one ancestor before him, and be stripped of his lands and titles. This helps to put into perspective the fight that Alina and her husband put up to keep their inheritance of Gower.

During her childhood, Alina would have moved between Oystermouth and Swansea Castles in Gower, and back and forth to the estates in Bramber. Later she would have also spent a lot of time in her husband's various estates, especially in the north of England. Their first child, John, was not born until 1310, when Alina was nineteen and John twenty four, and he was born in Yorkshire.[21]

Chapter 2 – Family History[22]

Gillaume de Briouze (d.c.1085) is recorded as a companion of William the Conqueror in lists of those present at the Battle of Hastings. The Briouze name comes from the village of Briouze-Saint-Gervais and their estate was in southern Normandy[23], but he was also awarded estates in conquered England which made him one of the twenty wealthiest barons there. He had the whole of the Rape of Bramber, one of the six north-south sections into which West Sussex was divided[24], and built Bramber Castle, of which little now remains. His name was anglicised as William de Braose, the first of that name, which was later spelled Breos or Breuse. Locals in Gower today pronounce it 'Bruce'.

His son Philip (d.c.1150) became Lord of Builth and Radnor, the first de Breos holdings in Wales. For a while the family's fortunes continued well. The fourth Lord of Bramber, another William (d.1211), fought alongside King Richard at Chalus in 1199, when Richard was fatally wounded. William supported Prince John's claim to the throne and was richly rewarded, becoming one of the richest and most powerful men in the country. Indeed it was King John who gave him Gower, in 1203.[25]

However, his fall began almost immediately, and the de Breos family won and lost and won Gower again from the king, and then lost and regained Gower from the Prince of Gwynedd, and all within seventeen years![26] Things became more stable for the de Breos family after that, until William (1261-1326), Alina's father, inherited the estates in 1291.[27]

William's father married three times, and he had at least five siblings, but William was the eldest son, and would have inherited everything unless special provision was made. The main estate given to the second son was Tetbury in Gloucestershire, and possibly other minor manors were given to other children, but the bulk of the estates came to William.[28]

Alina's immediate family tree

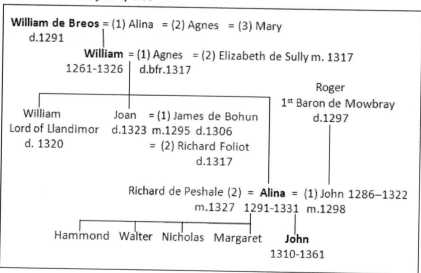

At the time of his inheritance, the main estates were Bramber and Gower, but William seems to have spent a lot of time in Gower, and rebuilt Oystermouth Castle in stone, which he preferred to live in, although Swansea Castle was the main seat of

Gower.[29] However, it is possible that Swansea Castle was in some disrepair, as the whole town was sacked and burned just over fifty years before, by Rhys ap Maredudd (c.1250-1292) in a Welsh uprising.

The aristocracy spent a lot of their time fighting, either on battlefields or in the law courts. When they weren't away fighting for the king or fighting the Welsh, they were fighting each other. In England, each baron or lord was given lands that they held under the king, but in Wales the king had effectively said that they could have any land they could take and hold, and rule them as they wished.[30] So when the Welsh weren't attacking them to drive out the invaders, they were attacking each other in an attempt to increase their estates.

This, then, was Alina's legacy. She came from illustrious ancestors, down to relative poverty. The estates of Gower and Bramber, no doubt, produced a good income, but this had to cover not only the family's living expenses but also her father and grandfather's debts, and the cost of continually raising men to fight for the king.

Chapter 3 - Inheritances

William de Breos (1261-1326) inherited Gower and Bramber from his father, and you would expect his son William to inherit after him. But his son died before him, in 1320, leaving no heirs. So William decided to settle Gower on Alina.[31]

William's second child was a daughter, Joan, who married James de Bohun of Midhurst in 1295, not long after Alina was born. There is no record of any lands being promised to her, and we assume she would have gone to live on her husband's estates. Joan died in 1323.[32]

That left Alina as William's only heir, along with her husband John de Mowbray. De Mowbray, however, did not trust his father-in-law and made a contract with him that guaranteed their succession.[33] But even then Alina's inheritance of Bramber and Gower was by no means safe. Her father had long term money troubles and was always looking for ways to raise money or avoid paying it out.

In 1320, on the death of his son, William arranged to sell the reversion of Gower to Humphrey de Bohun, the earl of Hereford.[34] A reversion was the right to inherit if William's heirs died childless. This is strange, because Alina had had a son in 1310.[35] De Bohun wanted Gower for his son after Alina's death. This sale would not have been a problem legally - although Alina and John would not have been happy - but William also sold the reversion of Gower to two other marcher lords, Roger Mortimer of Chirk and Roger Mortimer of Wigmore. William was getting into very dangerous waters. Things came to a head when he sold Gower outright to Hugh le Despenser the Younger.[36]

Alina and John saw their Gower inheritance disappearing. The reversion only applied to their heirs, but selling Gower outright meant it would never come to them. John de Mowbray decided to take matters into his own hands, and took control of Swansea Castle.[37] This probably did not involve force, but taking possession of the official seals.[38] Whatever it took, the king was not going to accept it, for two reasons.

At the end of the thirteenth century, King Edward I had finally conquered the Welsh, but he wanted to keep the Marcher Lords in submission as well. They had come to believe that they were a law unto themselves[39], but Edward wanted to make it clear that they only ruled with his permission. Part of the purpose of his journey around Wales after the conquest was to face down the Marcher Lords whom he visited. His son, Edward II, felt even more threatened by them. Edward I was a champion, called 'the best lance in the world'[40] and 'the Hammer of the Scots.'[41] His son Edward II was the complete opposite.

The other reason was Hugh le Despenser the Younger (1286-1326). Edward, although married and with a son, enjoyed many male 'friends'. His special favourite was Piers Gaveston, and when he was taken from him, Hugh le Despenser, known as Despenser the Younger, became his new favourite.[42] Hugh le Despenser the Elder (1262-1326), was his father. The court was appalled at his homosexual behaviour, and since the prevailing belief was that the king could do no wrong, Despenser was blamed for corrupting him. On the king's part, Despenser could do no wrong, and Despenser took every advantage.

In 1317 Despenser had obtained by marriage the lordship of Glamorgan, which bordered Gower. In quick succession he secured Gwynllŵg, Usk, Dryslwyn, Cantref Mawr and Emlyn (now known as Newcastle Emlyn).[43] He was known as the most covetous of the Marcher Lords ever.[44] He wanted Gower, so that the River Loughor would be the border between his lands and the Lancaster lordship of Kidwelly.[45] So when John de Mowbray seized what Despenser had paid for, Despenser persuaded the king to seize it.[46] Mowbray declared that the king's authority did not apply in the Marches, and the other barons agreed. They guarded their Marcher rights jealously and would not allow the king to impose his rule there.[47]

On 26th October 1320, a band of men were sent to take back Swansea Castle, but they were met by an armed band of Welsh-men in St Thomas who refused to allow them to cross the River Tawe.[48] (The Welsh supported John de Mowbray because of their hatred of Despenser, who had executed without trial the rebel leader Llewellyn Bren.[49]) On 13th November a larger force from the king's own household were sent, and reached Swansea Castle without opposition. However, the Marcher Lords and other barons who were not happy with the king's favouritism, viewed this action as a challenge to their autonomy, and rose in revolt.[50] That local rebellion, like a rolling snowball, gathered other barons in a country-wide uprising against a weak and distrusted king.

Led by Humphrey de Bohun of Hereford and Thomas, the earl of Lancaster, and despite the king forbidding assemblies[51], they met to discuss their options, and on 4th May 1321 they attacked the Despenser lands in the Marches. (Lancaster was the king's cousin, but alarmed at the politics at court.[52]) Within nine days, Newport, Cardiff, and Gower fell, and the main Despenser holdings were devastated.[53] The seneschal of Gower, John Iweyn, refused to join the rebels and was later found to have been working for the Despensers.[54] This was no local revolt, but a full scale civil war, between the Marcher and northern lords, supported by many knights from the south west, against those loyal to the king in the south and east.[55]

In August, having proved their strength, the king met with them in parliament where they brought a catalogue of charges against Hugh le Despenser and his father. They accused them of usurping royal power, refusing anyone access to the king unless they were present, replacing good officials with corrupt ones, and the murder of Llewellyn Bren, among other charges. The king was advised that he had no choice but to give in to their demands. The two Despensers were banished, and the barons were pardoned.[56]

John de Mowbray had Gower returned to him, and finding out about Iweyn's treachery, had him executed.[57]

Chapter 4 - Schemes

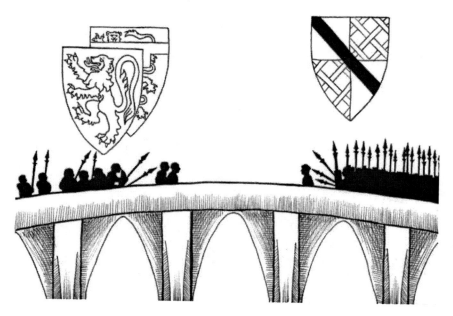

All would seem to be well. A weak king had been made to give up those who were exercising undue influence on him, they had been banished, and John and Alina had regained Gower. However, it was not to last for long. In October of 1321, provoked by the constable of Leeds Castle's wife's slight of the queen, the king launched a counter offensive against the barons, and declared everyone who opposed him a traitor.[58] He was not prepared to allow them to best him and insisted on reasserting himself. And he wanted his favourite back. In November he gave orders for Rhys ap Gruffydd, a Welsh leader who supported the king, to attack the rebels in West Wales. By February he had taken Gower for the king.[59]

Despenser the Elder had gone quietly into exile abroad, but his son Hugh le Despenser the Younger took to the seas as a pirate, and robbed merchant ships up and down the English Channel.[60] He was almost as much of a menace in exile as he had been at court. Many claimed that his actions were condoned by the king, and that he was operating out of the Cinque Ports. It wasn't long before Edward had recalled both Despensers and arranged to have their condemnation revoked.[61]

Edward's army marched across the River Severn at Shrewsbury in January 1322, and many of the barons surrendered without a fight. Some of the main leaders, including the Earl of Hereford and John de Mowbray, escaped north and joined the Earl of Lancaster, a close friend of the Mowbray family and cousin to the king, at Pontefract, to set up a resistance, and once the king had worked his way through the Marches he headed north to meet them.[62]

The rebels were expecting to meet up with reinforcements, but due to a breakdown in communication, the meeting didn't happen. When they met the king's forces they were defeated, at the battle of Boroughbridge in Yorkshire on 16th March 1322.[63] The bridge in question was a major crossing where the Great North Road crossed the River Ure. The royal forces took control of the bridge, putting the rebel forces, under Lancaster and Hereford, at a disadvantage. There was no other way across the river and they were being pursued. Without their reinforcements, the rebels were outnumbered. The battle was short and decisive, and the rebel leaders were captured, except for Hereford, who was killed.[64]

The rebel leaders were taken to York to be tried and executed.[65] Lancaster escaped a more grisly death due to his royal blood, and was simply beheaded[66], but Mowbray was subjected to the full wrath of the king. He was drawn and hung and his body displayed in chains, and the king refused to allow his body to be taken down for three years. He was eventually buried in the Dominican friary at York.[67]

Alina's hopes for her inheritance were dashed, and with her husband condemned as a traitor to the crown, Alina and her son John fled by boat to Ilfracombe, North Devon. They were pursued and captured, taken to London and imprisoned in the Tower of

London.[68] Alina was thirty one years old, and her son was only twelve. Her father William was sixty one, a great age in those days.

The Despensers took full advantage of their return to grace, and the defeat of the rebels. The king was persuaded to grant them many of the rebels' lands. Hugh le Despenser the Younger in particular acquired enough land to put him in control of the whole of South Wales. He had an income from his Welsh lands of £4000 a year, with another £1000 a year from lands of which he was custodian.[69] That would be worth over £1.6m today. From this time onwards, he virtually ruled England on behalf of Edward II.[70]

Despenser had paid William de Breos, Alina's father, £10,000 for Gower, but since the king had confiscated it and given it to Despenser, he wanted his money back. Of course, William didn't have it, and with his son-in-law dead and disgraced and his daughter in the Tower, he was a broken man.

Despenser had finally got hold of Gower, but that wasn't all he wanted. He had his eye on Gwent, owned by his widowed sister-in-law Elizabeth de Burgh, and persuaded the king to allow him to exchange it for Gower.[71] He persuaded her to make the exchange by imprisoning her until she agreed! He gave orders for Gower to be devastated before it was handed over. Having acquired Gwent, he then persuaded William de Breos to go to court and claim that Gower had been illegally acquired, and when it was returned to him, he promptly gave it to Despenser.[72] Thus Despenser ended up with both Gwent *and* Gower.

Chapter 5 - Undone

The two Despensers' hold over the king not only caused resentment among the barons and the court, but, understandably, with the queen. Isabella was the sister of the king of France, Charles IV. When a dispute arose between England and France over Gascony, Isabella managed to persuade the king to send her to her brother to make peace, and so escaped from court and from England.[73]

The Despensers may have been good at scheming, but proved less skilled at administration. In May 1325 Isabella negotiated that either the king or his son would go to France and pay homage to Charles IV for Gascony, and the Despensers, fearful of losing their hold over the king, agreed to send Prince Edward rather than his father. Once Isabella had her son with her, there was nothing to stop her working against the Despensers and the king.[74] She wrote to the king that neither she nor her son would return to his court as long as the younger Despenser was there. She said that her marriage was broken and she would live as a widow until the Despensers were gone.[75]

While in France, Isabella met, and fell in love with, Roger Mortimer, an English exile. Roger Mortimer was one of the barons who rebelled against Edward II, and when he surrendered he was imprisoned in the Tower of London. He managed to escape by drugging his guards, and fled to France.[76] Although for different reasons, they were both in opposition to the king, and both believed he was bad for England. They canvassed for support and gathered a growing band of men who were also disenchanted with the king and his administration.[77] They began to raise an army to invade.

In September 1326 Isabella and Mortimer landed in the south of England with 700 mercenaries.[78] Edward was amazed at the small size of their army and immediately attempted to raise a large force to crush them. To his surprise, many of the barons refused him.[79] Many joined the queen. The invasion quickly had too much support and became too big to stop.

The king and Despenser the Younger soon realised that they had too little support, and could not prevail against Mortimer and Isabella. In October they left London and took refuge in Gloucester, and then fled to South Wales, where they hoped to mount a defence in Despenser's lands. When the king fled, he took the great seal of England and a considerable amount of silver with him. Mortimer was concerned that he would attempt to set up a government in exile. In order to get from Gloucester to Wales, the king went by sea. Mortimer argued that the king had left the country and not appointed a regent, so technically there was no royal authority in England.

Mortimer and Isabella took advantage of this, and appointed Prince Edward as regent.[80] He was appointed on the day Bristol fell to their army, and in Bristol they captured Despenser's father. He was accused of a list of crimes, including encouraging the illegal government of his son, enriching himself at the expense of others, and despoiling the Church. He was hanged and beheaded at the Bristol Gallows.[81]

Henry of Lancaster was sent to Wales after Edward and the younger Despenser. When they had arrived at Cardiff, they were still unable to raise an army, and even their servants deserted them, leaving them with just a few retainers. As Lancaster pursued them, they fled westward, arriving at Neath Abbey.[82] From there the king sent his treasure, papers and other valuables to Swansea Castle, where he had appointed John de Langton as seneschal and authorised him to see to the defence of the town.[83] On 16th November 1326 they were captured in open country.[84] Most of their retainers were released, Despenser and two others were sent to Isabella and Mortimer at Hereford and the king was taken by Lancaster to his fortress in the Midlands, Kenilworth Castle.[85]

Revenge against Despenser was brutal, and a huge crowd gathered to see him executed, after a quick trial. They were particularly angered and disgusted at what they regarded as his homosexual corruption of the king. He was forced to wear the coat of arms of Gilbert de Clare, to signify that he owed his greatness to his wife and was nothing in himself. He was drawn, hung fifty feet high with his head between the prongs of a fork and jerked up and down until he was dead. Then he was beheaded and quartered and his bowels thrown into the fire.[86]

Other leading figures who had supported the king were also executed. The problem facing Mortimer and the queen was what to do with the king. The simplest thing would be execution, which would pass the throne to the prince, who could be controlled by Isabella, since he was only fourteen. But to execute him required a trial for treason, and they were not sure this would be possible. Many believed that the king was called by God and could not be removed by the people.

They initially decided to keep him imprisoned, and Isabella, with the great seal, was ruling in the name of the king, of herself, and of the prince, his heir.[87] But this was actually illegal, and could have been challenged. As long as the king was alive, there was also the chance that there would be an attempt to return him to the throne. In the end, Parliament recalled the House of Commons and, after much debate, they decided to ask the king to abdicate. They were not willing to depose him, but asked him to accept their decision.[88]

When Edward was informed of the charges against him, he wept. The list was very long, and he was shocked at the extent of it, and that the people hated him. He was accused of pursuing occupations unbecoming to a monarch and incompetence; of allowing others to govern him to the detriment of the people and Church and of not listening to good advice. He had lost Scotland and lands in Ireland and Gascony through failure of effective governance.[89] He had allowed nobles to be killed, disinherited, imprisoned and exiled; he had damaged the Church and imprisoned its representatives.[90] Many of the charges reflected Hugh le Despenser's influence on Edward.

The king agreed to abdicate in favour of his son, if the people would agree to accept him. The abdication was registered on 24th January 1327, and the following day was declared the first day of the reign of Edward III[91], even though he was only fourteen. Mortimer and Isabella were appointed as regents. Mortimer also took the title Earl of March.[92] From rebel in exile, Roger Mortimer had become effectively the king of England.[93]

When Edward was seventeen he led a coup against Mortimer and began his personal reign.[94] He was one of the most successful monarchs of the Middle Ages, and reigned for fifty years.

Chapter 6 - Restored

While all this was going on, Alina was imprisoned in the Tower of London. Life there could be as comfortable as you could afford to make it[95], however, Alina's father had money problems and her husband's inheritances had been confiscated. Later she was transferred to the custody of Hugh le Despenser the Elder, who made her life really miserable, presumably in revenge for her husband's actions, until she gave up to him the only inheritance remaining to her: the Sussex estates, including Bramber, that she had from her father.[96] Her son was permitted to inherit the Mowbray estates.

Her father, William de Breos, became increasingly frail and senile. He gave up almost everything in a frantic attempt to achieve her freedom. He died in 1326[97], and never saw her free.

With his death, the de Breos line ended. Alina was eventually freed in 1327, when Edward III became king, and the sentence on her husband was reversed at the same time.[98] She was thirty six and her son John was seventeen. In the first year of Edward's reign, an act of parliament was passed which returned lands to most of those who had been dispossessed by the Despensers. However, since the original transfer of Gower to Alina and John by William had not been approved by the king, this did not apply to Alina. She would have been left with nowhere to go, but the new king took pity on her, and gave her back Gower.[99] The gift was legalised on 1st March 1327.[100]

Within a year, she married Richard de Peshale, whom she had met while in the Tower.[101] It has not been possible to find out any information about de Peshale. They took up residence in Oystermouth Castle. Legend has it that the chapel block was built on Alina's instructions. It would be nice to think that she lived happily ever after, but almost immediately she had to commission an inquiry into a complaint made against her by one of her tenants.[102] Perhaps she ran her estate the way her father had.

She had four children in quick succession: Hammond, Walter, Nicholas, and Margaret, and died in 1331[103], only four years after her release from the Tower. Tradition has it that she was buried in St Mary's Church at Swansea[104], but no trace of her tomb has been found.[105] We know very little about these children, except that Hammond and Margaret both married and Hammond served in France in 1380 in the retinue of Hugh, Earl of Stafford.[106] We know more about her first child, John, who was the third Lord Mowbray.

John had been born at Hovingham in Yorkshire, in 1310[107], and when his father's friend Lancaster heard the news, he rewarded the messenger with twenty shillings, a considerable sum in those days. Later, Lancaster was witness to his father's grant of Hovingham and other lands to young John and his wife. John was heir to the baronies of Bramber and Gower, as well as the extensive Mowbray lands including Axholme.[108] We do know that he spent some of his time in Gower, because there are records of him making grants to the abbeys of Neath and Margam from Oystermouth Castle in 1334 and 1350.[109]

John was also responsible for repairing Swansea Castle, and probably added the arcading which can still be seen atop the south wall.[110] St Mary's Church was annexed to the Hospital of St David, founded by Bishop Henry de Gower, which was built with Alina's support,[111] on the current site of the Cross Keys public house (which may be in part of the original building). It is thought that John borrowed the bishop's masons, since the arcading on the castle wall closely resembles that on the bishop's palace at St Davids.[112]

He was a constant companion in arms of Edward III and raised men from Gower to fight for the king on many occasions. He fought in many French campaigns including the siege of Nantes in Brittany and the battle of Crécy, as well as in Scotland. Continuing the close link of his family with that of Lancaster, he married Joan Plantagenet, Henry of Lancaster's daughter, and later married Elisabeth de Vere, the Earl of Oxford's daughter.[113] He died in 1361.[114]

The intrigue does not end with the death of Alina. As mentioned in the previous chapter, Edward II, in his flight westwards, sent his valuables from Neath Abbey to Swansea Castle before he was captured. In the upheaval which followed, the valuables were temporarily forgotten; only temporarily however. In July 1331, about the same time as Alina's death, Richard de Peshale was commissioned by Edward III to investigate what happened to the king's goods and treasure, which was estimated to be worth £63,000 (about £29m today). It included gold and silver plates, coins and jewellery, fine clothing, arms, armour, and horses. Many of the king's papers were found.[115] After three inquiries about £3000 worth was recovered[116], and in April 1336 a Royal Commission sought to bring to justice those who had stolen the rest. It does not appear that anyone was convicted.[117] Maybe William's debts were paid after all.

Conclusion

Alina de Breos was born into an aristocratic family much reduced from their former glories, but her marriage to John de Mowbray was set to remedy all that. Heir to substantial lands and friends of the house of Lancaster who were related to the king, the future looked bright for the Mowbrays. And she did have over twenty years of good life with John.

But her father, who had continued to get the Breos family's finances into trouble, managed to ruin their good life. John de Mowbray was heir to a large number of estates and well respected as a fighting man, but he guarded jealously what he believed was his. Or perhaps he was guarding what was his wife's. In an attempt to hang on to one estate out of many, he tapped in to a well of resentment rising across the country.

Edward II was a sharp contrast to his father, and his behaviour upset everyone, except those who benefitted. The Marcher Lords had been allowed to rule in Wales as they pleased, and proved impossible to reign in. This powder keg was lit by John de Mowbray's little revolt, and the resultant uprising led to the fall of the king. Although it was the queen who landed with an army, it was the simmering rebellion which led the barons to join the queen instead of the king.

Alina's fairy tale ended in the Tower of London, her husband disgraced and executed, and Despenser the Elder making her life a misery. She was relieved by the fall of the king, and restored to Gower by an act of mercy by the new king. Even her happiness at her new marriage was short. She died only four years after her release.

Her son John inherited the Mowbray estates and the barony, and made a name for himself. He eventually inherited Gower, and although he spent most of his time in the north, he is recorded as staying at Oystermouth Castle when he visited Gower.[118] Alina's other children were de Peshale's. The name of de Breos died with Alina's father.

Bibliography

Bartlett, Robert, *Gerald of Wales: A Voice of the Middle Ages* (2006)

Bartlett, Robert, *The Hanged Man: a story of miracle, memory and colonialism in the Middle Ages* (2004)

Brabbs, Derry, *England's Heritage*

Draisey, Derek, *A History of Gower* (2002)

Ericson, Carolly, *Brief Lives of the English Monarchs* (2007)

Evans, Edith, *Swansea Castle and the medieval town* (1983)

Glamorgan Gwent Archaeological Trust: File ref 471W

Herbert, Trevor & Jones, Gareth Elwyn, (ed.), *Edward I and Wales* (1988)

Hull, Lise, *Castles of Glamorgan: Monuments in the landscape Vol XII, a Logaston Guide (2007)*

Jones, W H, *The History of Swansea and the Lordship of Gower Vol.I* (1920)

Jones, W H, *The History of Swansea and the Lordship of Gower Vol.II* (1992)

King, Edmund, *Medieval England: from hastings to bosworth* (2005)

Lewis-Stemple, John, (ed.), *England: The Autobiography; 2000 years of English history by those who saw it happen* (2006)

Lieberman, Max, *The March of Wales 1067-1300: A Borderland of Medieval Britain* (2008)

McKisack, May, *The Oxford History of England, the Fourteenth Century 1307-1399* (1959)

Mortimer, Ian, *The Perfect King: The Life of Edward III, Father of the English Nation* (2007)

Royal Commission on Ancient Monuments of Wales, *An inventory of the ancient monuments in Glamorgan: Volume III (Part 1a) Medieval secular monuments: The early castles from the Norman conquest to 1217* (1991)

Royal Commission on Ancient Monuments of Wales, *An inventory of the ancient monuments in Glamorgan: Volume III (Part 1b) Medieval secular monuments: The later castles from 1217 to the present* (2001)

Rubin, Miri, *The Hollow Crown: A History of Britain in the Late Middle Ages* (2005)

Thomas, W S K, *The History of Swansea* (1990)

Walker, David, *Medieval Wales* (1990)

Online Resources:

Archer, Rowena E, 'Mowbray, John (I), second Lord Mowbray (1286–1322), magnate', *Oxford Dictionary of National Biography*, Oxford University Press, Sept 2004; online edn, Jan 2008
http://www.oxforddnb.com/view/article/19450

De Braose website
http://freespace.virgin.net/doug.thompson/BraoseWeb/family/

Carter, Rachelle, *Marriage in Medieval Times*,
www.dfwx.com/medieval_cult.html

Hamilton, J S, *Despenser, Hugh, the younger, first Lord Despenser (d.1326), administrator and royal favourite*, © Oxford University Press 2004-9

Hull, Marvin, www.castles-of-britain.com/castlezb.htm © 2001-2008

http://library.thinkquest.org/12834/text/distaffside.html

www.oxforddnb.com/view/article/19450

www.theheritagetrail.co.uk/castles/bramber%20castle.htm

http://thepeerage.com, *The Complete Peerage of England, Scotland, Ireland, Great Britain and the United Kingdom, Extant, Extinct or Dormant, new ed.*, 13 volumes in 14 (1910-1959; reprint in 6 volumes, Gloucester, U.K.: Alan Sutton Publishing, 2000)

Other Resources:

Glamorgan Gwent Archaeological Trust

The Borough of Swansea Local Historical Records

CADW Ancient Monuments Record Forms for Swansea Castle & Oystermouth Castle

Oystermouth Castle, Swansea, Conservation and Management Plan

Endnotes

[1] Hull, Lise, *Castles of Glamorgan (Monuments in the Landscape, Volume XII, a Logaston Guide)*, p.219

[2] Evans, Edith, *Swansea Castle and the medieval town*, p.3

[3] Hull, Lise, *Castles of Glamorgan (Monuments in the Landscape, Volume XII, a Logaston Guide)*, p.219

[4] Royal Commission on Ancient Monuments of Wales, *An inventory of the ancient monuments in Glamorgan: Volume III (Part 1b) Medieval secular monuments: The later castles from 1217 to the present*, p.349

[5] Hull, Lise, *Castles of Glamorgan (Monuments in the Landscape, Volume XII, a Logaston Guide)*, p.167
Oystermouth Castle, Swansea, Conservation & Management Plan, p.7

[6] G.E. Cokayne; with Vicary Gibbs, H.A. Doubleday, Geoffrey H. White, Duncan Warrand and Lord Howard de Walden, editors, *The Complete Peerage of England, Scotland, Ireland, Great Britain and the United Kingdom, Extant, Extinct or Dormant, new ed.*, 13 volumes in 14 (1910-1959; reprint in 6 volumes, Gloucester, U.K.: Alan Sutton Publishing, 2000), volume II, page 303. Hereinafter cited as *The Complete Peerage*

[7] www.theheritagetrail.co.uk/castles/bramber%20castle.htm

[8] De Braose family website
http://freespace.virgin.net/doug.thompson/BraoseWeb/family/

[9] Davies, R R, 'Edward I and Wales', *Edward I and Wales* edited by Herbert, Trevor & Jones, Gareth Elwyn, p.1
Lieberman, Max, *The March of Wales 1067-1300: A Borderland of Medieval Britain*, p.1

[10] Bartlett, Robert, *Gerald of Wales: A Voice of the Middle Ages*, p.19

[11] Glamorgan Gwent Archaeological Society: File ref 471W Close Rolls Vol 1288-1296 p.163

[12] De Braose family website
http://freespace.virgin.net/doug.thompson/BraoseWeb/family/

[13] Walker, David, *Medieval Wales*, p.50ff

[14] Lieberman, Max, *The March of Wales 1067-1300: A Borderland of Medieval Britain*, p.38

[15] Jones, W H, *The History of Swansea and the Lordship of Gower Vol.I*

[16] Draisey, Derek, *A History of Gower*, p.65

[17] Bartlett, Robert, *The Hanged Man*, p. 89
De Braose family website
http://freespace.virgin.net/doug.thompson/BraoseWeb/family/

[18] Evans, Edith, *Swansea Castle and the medieval town*, p.14

[19] Hull, Marvin, *Medieval Women* © 2001-2008, http://www.castles-of-britain.com/castlezb.htm

http://library.thinkquest.org/12834/text/distaffside.html

Carter, Rachelle, Amt, Emilie, Marriage in Medieval Times, *Women's Lives in Medieval Europe,* New York, Routledge (1993)

http://www.dfwx.com/medieval_cult.html

[20] De Braose family website

http://freespace.virgin.net/doug.thompson/BraoseWeb/family/

[21] Archer, Rowena E, 'Mowbray, John (I), second Lord Mowbray (1286–1322), magnate', *Oxford Dictionary of National Biography*, Oxford University Press, Sept 2004; online edn, Jan 2008

http://www.oxforddnb.com/view/article/19450

[22] The bulk of this chapter taken from:

De Braose family website

http://freespace.virgin.net/doug.thompson/BraoseWeb/family/

Walker, David, *Medieval Wales*, p.50ff

Draisey, Derek, *A History of Gower*, p.43-64

[23] Draisey, Derek, *A History of Gower*, p.43

[24] Bartlett, Robert, *The Hanged Man*, p. 86

[25] Bartlett, Robert, *The Hanged Man*, p. 87

[26] Bartlett, Robert, *The Hanged Man*, p. 73

[27] Bartlett, Robert, *The Hanged Man*, p. 60-61

[28] Bartlett, Robert, *The Hanged Man*, p. 98

[29] *Oystermouth Castle, Swansea, Conservation & Management Plan*, p.6

[30] Smith, Llinos Beverley, 'The Governance of Edwardian Wales', *Edward I and Wales* edited by Herbert, Trevor & Jones, Gareth Elwyn, p.76

Bartlett, Robert, *The Hanged Man*, p. 90-91, 93

[31] Bartlett, Robert, *The Hanged Man*, p. 138

[32] De Braose family website

http://freespace.virgin.net/doug.thompson/BraoseWeb/family/

[33] Draisey, Derek, *A History of Gower*, p.72

[34] Bartlett, Robert, *The Hanged Man*, p. 139

[35] De Braose family website

http://freespace.virgin.net/doug.thompson/BraoseWeb/family/

[36] De Braose family website

http://freespace.virgin.net/doug.thompson/BraoseWeb/family/

Mortimer, Ian, *The Perfect King, The Life of Edward III, Father of the English Nation*, p.30

Hamilton, J S, *Despenser, Hugh, the younger, first Lord Despenser (d. 1326), administrator and royal favourite,* © Oxford University Press 2004–9

Draisey, Derek, *A History of Gower*, p.72

[37] Hamilton, J S, *Despenser, Hugh, the younger, first Lord Despenser (d. 1326), administrator and royal favourite,* © Oxford University Press 2004–9

[38] Gabb, Gerald, in conversation

[39] Smith, Llinos Beverley, 'The Governance of Edwardian Wales', *Edward I and Wales* edited by Herbert, Trevor & Jones, Gareth Elwyn, p.76
Bartlett, Robert, *The Hanged Man*, p. 90-91, 93

[40] Lewis-Stemple, J, (ed.), *England The Autobiography*, p.61

[41] Lewis-Stemple, J, (ed.), *England The Autobiography*, p.62
Bartlett, Robert, *The Hanged Man*, p. 23

[42] Walker, David, *Medieval Wales*, p.56-7
Ericson, Carolly, *Brief Lives of the English Monarchs*, p.105

[43] Walker, David, *Medieval Wales*, p.56-7, 163

[44] Walker, David, *Medieval Wales*, p.56

[45] McKisack, May, *The Oxford History of England, the Fourteenth Century 1307-1399*, p.59

[46] Draisey, Derek, *A History of Gower*, p.73

[47] Smith, Llinos Beverley, 'The Governance of Edwardian Wales', *Edward I and Wales* edited by Herbert, Trevor & Jones, Gareth Elwyn, p.76

[48] Evans, Edith, *Swansea Castle and the medieval town*, p.10

[49] http://www.cardiffworld.com/info/History-of-cardiff/Mediaeval-Cardiff.html

[50] De Braose family website
http://freespace.virgin.net/doug.thompson/BraoseWeb/family/
McKisack, May, *The Oxford History of England, the Fourteenth Century 1307-1399*, p.59

[51] McKisack, May, *The Oxford History of England, the Fourteenth Century 1307-1399*, p.61

[52] Rubin, Miri, *The Hollow Crown: A History of Britain in the Late Middle Ages*, p.30

[53] Rubin, Miri, *The Hollow Crown: A History of Britain in the Late Middle Ages*, p.35
McKisack, May, *The Oxford History of England, the Fourteenth Century 1307-1399*, p.61

[54] Royal Commission on Ancient Monuments of Wales, *An inventory of the ancient monuments in Glamorgan: Volume III (Part 1b) Medieval secular monuments: The later castles from 1217 to the present*, p.349

[55] Hamilton, J S, *Despenser, Hugh, the younger, first Lord Despenser (d. 1326), administrator and royal favourite*, © Oxford University Press 2004–9
Mortimer, Ian, *The Perfect King, The Life of Edward III, Father of the English Nation*, p.30

[56] Hamilton, J S, *Despenser, Hugh, the younger, first Lord Despenser (d. 1326), administrator and royal favourite*, © Oxford University Press 2004–9
Bartlett, Robert, *The Hanged Man*, p.140

McKisack, May, *The Oxford History of England, the Fourteenth Century 1307-1399*, p.64

[57] Royal Commission on Ancient Monuments of Wales, *An inventory of the ancient monuments in Glamorgan: Volume III (Part 1a) Medieval secular monuments: The early castles from the Norman conquest to 1217*, p.266ff

Draisey, Derek, *A History of Gower*, p.73

[58] McKisack, May, *The Oxford History of England, the Fourteenth Century 1307-1399*, p.64

[59] Draisey, Derek, *A History of Gower*, p.73

[60] King, Edmund, *Medieval England from hastings to bosworth*, p.181

[61] McKisack, May, *The Oxford History of England, the Fourteenth Century 1307-1399*, p.65

[62] McKisack, May, *The Oxford History of England, the Fourteenth Century 1307-1399*, p.65

[63] Draisey, Derek, *A History of Gower*, p.73

[64] McKisack, May, *The Oxford History of England, the Fourteenth Century 1307-1399*, p.66

[65] King, Edmund, *Medieval England from hastings to bosworth*, p.182

[66] Rubin, Miri, *The Hollow Crown: A History of Britain in the Late Middle Ages*, p.35

McKisack, May, *The Oxford History of England, the Fourteenth Century 1307-1399*, p.65

[67] Jones, W H, *The History of Swansea and the Lordship of Gower Vol.I*, p.334ff

Mortimer, Ian, *The Perfect King, The Life of Edward III, Father of the English Nation*, p.31

Bartlett, Robert, *The Hanged Man*, p.140

[68] Jones, W H, *The History of Swansea and the Lordship of Gower Vol.I*, p.334ff

http://www.stepneyrobarts.co.uk/12870.htm

[69] Walker, David, *Medieval Wales*, p.56-7

[70] Draisey, Derek, *A History of Gower*, p.75

[71] Jones, W H, *The History of Swansea and the Lordship of Gower Vol.I*, p.334ff

[72] Draisey, Derek, *A History of Gower*, p.74

[73] Lewis-Stemple, John, (ed.), *England The Autobiography*, p.64

Walker, David, *Medieval Wales*, p.56-7

McKisack, May, *The Oxford History of England, the Fourteenth Century 1307-1399*, p.81

Ericson, Carolly, *Brief Lives of the English Monarchs*, p.107

[74] Walker, David, *Medieval Wales*, p.56-7

Ericson, Carolly, *Brief Lives of the English Monarchs*, p.107-108

[75] McKisack, May, *The Oxford History of England, the Fourteenth Century 1307-1399*, p.82

[76] Ericson, Carolly, *Brief Lives of the English Monarchs*, p.107
Lieberman, Max, *The March of Wales 1067-1300: A Borderland of Medieval Britain*, p.6

[77] King, Edmund, *Medieval England from hastings to bosworth*, p.185

[78] Draisey, Derek, *A History of Gower*, p.75

[79] Walker, David, *Medieval Wales*, p.56-7
Ericson, Carolly, *Brief Lives of the English Monarchs*, p.108

[80] Mortimer, Ian, *The Perfect King, The Life of Edward III, Father of the English Nation*, p.49

[81] Walker, David, *Medieval Wales*, p.56-7
McKisack, May, *The Oxford History of England, the Fourteenth Century 1307-1399*, p.85-86

[82] Walker, David, *Medieval Wales*. p.56-7

[83] Draisey, Derek, *A History of Gower*, p.75

[84] Jones, W H, *The History of Swansea and the Lordship of Gower Vol.I*, p.334ff
McKisack, May, *The Oxford History of England, the Fourteenth Century 1307-1399*, p.86

[85] Mortimer, Ian, *The Perfect King, The Life of Edward III, Father of the English Nation*, p.50

[86] *Caerphilly Chronicle*,
www.caerphilly.gov.uk/chronicle/english/diggingdeeper/famousfaces/hughledespenseryounger.htm

[87] McKisack, May, *The Oxford History of England, the Fourteenth Century 1307-1399*, p.88

[88] McKisack, May, *The Oxford History of England, the Fourteenth Century 1307-1399*, p.90

[89] Ericson, Carolly, *Brief Lives of the English Monarchs*, p.109
King, Edmund, *Medieval England: from hastings to bosworth*, p.186

[90] McKisack, May, *The Oxford History of England, the Fourteenth Century 1307-1399*, p.90

[91] McKisack, May, *The Oxford History of England, the Fourteenth Century 1307-1399*, p.91

[92] King, Edmund, *Medieval England: from hastings to bosworth*, p.187

[93] Ericson, Carolly, *Brief Lives of the English Monarchs*, p.112-113

[94] Ericson, Carolly, *Brief Lives of the English Monarchs*, p.113

[95] Brabbs, Derry, *England's Heritage*, p.238

[96] Jones, W H, *The History of Swansea and the Lordship of Gower Vol.I*, p.334ff
Bartlett, Robert, *The Hanged Man*, p. 141
Draisey, Derek, *A History of Gower*, p.73

[97] De Braose family website
http://freespace.virgin.net/doug.thompson/BraoseWeb/family/

Draisey, Derek, *A History of Gower*, p.74
[98] Archer, Rowena E, 'Mowbray, John (I), second Lord Mowbray (1286–1322), magnate', *Oxford Dictionary of National Biography*, Oxford University Press, Sept 2004; online edn, Jan 2008 http://www.oxforddnb.com/view/article/19450
[99] Bartlett, Robert, *The Hanged Man*, p. 141
[100] Draisey, Derek, *A History of Gower*, p.75
Jones, W H, *The History of Swansea and the Lordship of Gower Vol.II*, p.9
[101] De Braose family website
http://freespace.virgin.net/doug.thompson/BraoseWeb/family/
[102] Draisey, Derek, *A History of Gower*, p.75
[103] De Braose family website
http://freespace.virgin.net/doug.thompson/BraoseWeb/family/
[104] Draisey, Derek, *A History of Gower*, p.75
[105] Jones, W H, *The History of Swansea and the Lordship of Gower Vol.II*, p.10
[106] De Braose family website
http://freespace.virgin.net/doug.thompson/BraoseWeb/family/
[107] Weir Alison, *Britain's Royal Family: A Complete Genealogy* (1999), p.77
http://thepeerage.com/p10688.htm#i106878
[108] De Braose family website
http://freespace.virgin.net/doug.thompson/BraoseWeb/family/
[109] Jones, W H, *The History of Swansea and the Lordship of Gower Vol.II*, p.13
[110] Jones, W H, *The History of Swansea and the Lordship of Gower Vol.II*, p.13
[111] Thomas, W S K, *The History of Swansea*, p28-9
[112] Draisey, Derek, *A History of Gower*, p.77-79
Evans, Edith, *Swansea Castle and the medieval town*, p.34-35
[113] Weir, Alison, *Britain's Royal Family: A Complete Genealogy* (1999), p.77
http://thepeerage.com/p10688.htm#i106878
[114] De Braose family website
http://freespace.virgin.net/doug.thompson/BraoseWeb/family/
[115] Jones, W H, *The History of Swansea and the Lordship of Gower Vol.II*, p.3
[116] Jones, W H, *The History of Swansea and the Lordship of Gower Vol.II*, p.3-5
[117] Draisey, Derek, *A History of Gower*, p.75-76
Jones, W H, *The History of Swansea and the Lordship of Gower Vol.II*, p.6
[118] Royal Commission on Ancient Monuments of Wales, *An inventory of the ancient monuments in Glamorgan: Volume III (Part 1b) Medieval secular monuments: The later castles from 1217 to the present*, p.245